The Illustrated History of

Leader of the Pack

GW00659446

Douglas
MOTORCYCLES

Harold Briercliffe & Eric Brockway

Foulis

Haynes

A FOULIS motorcycling book

Published by:
Haynes Publishing Group
Sparkford Nr. Yeovil Somerset BA22 7JJ England

Haynes Publications Inc
861 Lawrence Drive Newbury Park California 91320 USA

British Library cataloguing in publication Data
Briercliffe, Harold, 1910–
The illustrated history of Douglas motorcycles.
1. Douglas motorcycles, history
I. Title II. Brockway, Eric
629.2275

ISBN 0-85429-799-5

Library of Congress catalog card No: 90-82084

Editor: Jeff Clew
Cover Design: Camway Autographics
Layout Design: Chris Hull

Printed in England by J.H. Haynes & Co. Ltd.

Introduction

It is unusual for a large and at one time very successful motorcycle manufacturer to be located far away from Birmingham and Coventry, the hub of the industry, a distinction that makes Douglas almost unique. Even more unusual is the granting of a Royal Warrant endorsing the use of the company's products by members of the Royal Family, one of whom was later destined to become King, and by the Royal Household of Spain. Not surprisingly, in its heyday the Douglas motorcycle had become more a way of life than just a cold, inanimate means of transport. It enjoyed a production run that spanned fifty years and engendered a following that is still very much in evidence today.

William and Edward Douglas settled in Bristol during 1882 as foundrymen and it was not long before they became renowned for the quality of their castings. They established their works in Kingswood, on the outskirts of the city, but soon they went their separate ways, Edward being attracted by the boot and shoe trade for which the area was famous. Motorcycles at that time were in their infancy and it was through associations with Joseph Barter, the pioneer of the horizontally-opposed twin cylinder motorcycle engine, that the interest of William Douglas was aroused. Somewhat hesitatingly he took Barter under his wing to design and help build motorcycles under the Douglas name when the latter's own business had gone into liquidation. Thus, in 1907, the first Douglas motorcycle made its debut, another horizontally-opposed twin that was destined to become the hallmark of the company through virtually the whole of its existence.

The addition of a simple two-speed gearbox helped put the company on the map in terms of competition successes and it is probably a win in the 1912 Junior TT that brought the Douglas name to the attention of the War Office. The motorcycle was destined to play an important role in the 1914-18 War by providing transport for despatch riders in preference to the horse. A series of War Department contracts led to the manufacture of something like 25,000 machines for use by the armed forces, making Douglas (and Triumph) by far the largest suppliers. When motorcycling again got back onto a firm footing after the War, competition successes continued unabated, with riders of the calibre of Les Bailey, Cyril Pullin, Tom Sheard, Rex Judd and Freddie Dixon. A further landmark was that of producing the first 500cc motorcycle to exceed 100mph, which was further reinforced by two more TT wins, in the 1923 Senior and Sidecar events. The latter was the first of its kind to be held in the Isle of Man.

The newly-introduced EW model of 1925, although plagued initially by problems that led to heavy warranty claims, soon made a name for itself in trials-type competition events. By then, Prince Albert and Prince Henry had already joined the ranks of satisfied Douglas owners, affording the company some useful publicity, so it is fortunate that the disastrous fire at Kingswood in 1927 did not disrupt the company's business, long-term. In 1928 Douglas enjoyed yet another 'boom' when speedway racing was introduced to this country and spread like wildfire. With its low centre of gravity, long wheelbase and smooth power output, the Douglas proved ideal for this type of racing and for the next couple of years was virtually unbeatable. In 1929 alone, no less than 1,300 of these highly specialised machines had been sold.

Although the company was strong enough to be able to survive the slump of the late twenties and early thirties, it was forced into the manufacture of an additional lightweight single cylinder two-stroke in order to capture some of the lower end of the market. By this time William Douglas had relinquished his interest in the company, making what proved to be such an unfortunate decision that he had to buy it back again, mainly with his own money, to save it from liquidation. But it was only a temporary stay of execution. Not even the founder himself could prevent the inevitable. The company passed into other hands during mid-1935 and there was no longer a direct link with the Douglas family. The shock of this and the death of two of his sons brought about William's own demise in April 1937, at the age of 78.

By the outbreak of World War 2 the company was at a virtual sta   till as an anticipated contract for making Hispano Suiza aircraft engines under licence had not materialised As the manufacture of motorcycles was at a particularly low ebb too, there was no possibility of a contract for the manufacture of machines for the armed forces either. Deployment on munitions and similar war work provided the answer.

After the War, when the manufacture of motorcycles for the civilian market again became possible, the company came up with some interesting new designs that incorporated torsion bar rear suspension. Although they got off to a good start, recurring financial problems led to the appointment of an Official Receiver and from this point on, the yet again re-formed company never stood a real chance. Competition successes continued, albeit on a more modest scale, but even the decision to make the Vespa scooter under licence failed to bring about the desired revival as a major manufacturer. By 1955 the motorcycle range was down to one model, the Dragonfly, that represented an almost total redesign of the earlier 'Mark' series. The hoped-for 500cc model had never materialised, even though a prototype had been on display at the 1951 Motor Cycle Show. Further financial problems led to the acquisition of the company in 1956 by the Westinghouse Brake and Signal Company and in less than two years motorcycle and scooter production had come to an end. The production area was required for other purposes.

The Douglas name lingered on until June 1982, by which time small capacity Gilera motorcycles and a range of Vespa scooters and mopeds were being imported direct from Piaggio, their Italian-based manufacturer. No longer located at Kingswood, Douglas (Sales and Service) Ltd, operated from premises on the Fishponds Trading Estate. The end came when the company was acquired by Vespa (UK) Limited, a Heron Corporation Company, operating from the Heron Suzuki premises in Crawley, Sussex.

Despite its disappearance from the motorcycling scene the Douglas name remains as much in the mind of old motorcycle enthusiasts as it did when it was at its peak of production in the twenties. Its contribution to the motorcycle world was massive and if anything the role it played is being even more appreciated today.

Acknowledgements

The authors would like to acknowledge the help so willingly given by all who contributed in some way to the compilation of this book. Most of the photographs have originated from the old factory archives, which fortunately were saved and preserved by Eric Brockway, the company's last Director and General Manager. The balance was kindly provided by Graeme Brown of Godalming, the sole remaining Douglas Agent who has specialised in the Douglas marque for the whole of his working life, and a few by Jeff Clew from his personal collection. Each of them owns older models which are featured in the pages of this book.

Grateful thanks are also due to the London Douglas Motor Cycle Club, members of which have helped with the content of this book, sometimes quite unknowingly, and to Bendix Limited, the present occupants of the old Douglas factory in Kingswood. Bendix have kindly allowed access to their premises and to their Sports and Social Club whenever there has been need to commemorate Douglas anniversaries, as some of the latter day photographs will confirm. It is pleasing that they have shown such recognition of the name with which they have only tenuous links, to help perpetuate it.

Finally, tribute must be made to Kingswood Borough Council, who acted as hosts for members of the London Douglas Motor Cycle Club on the memorable occasion of the Club's Diamond Jubilee. Douglas enthusiasts everywhere must feel proud that this once famous name is still regarded with such pride and affection in the area from which most of its workforce once originated.

Whereas today the logo is regarded as the all-important key to a company's recognition, the motorcycle industry right from its early days tended to use transfers for the same purpose, which were affixed to the petrol tank and often to the steering head. Joseph Barter used this design for the horizontally-opposed twin cylinder motorcycles he manufactured under the trade name Fairy. The figurine presumably emphasises the lightness and delicate proportions of his diminutive 200cc engine, which also was very quiet in operation.

The early origins of the Douglas motorcycle are only too apparent in the Barter Fée, a name that was subsequently anglicised to Fairy when British-made motorcycles made their debut. As can be seen, the engine was little more than a clip-on unit fitted into a bicycle frame with a strengthened front fork. The primary drive was by chain to a simple countershaft which transmitted the final drive to the rear wheel by pulley and belt. Ignition was by trembler coil.

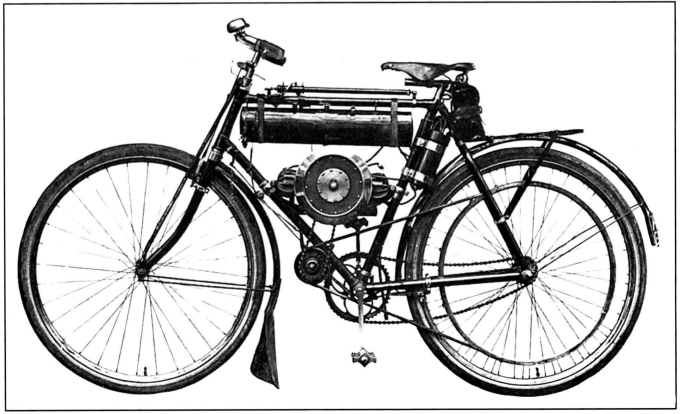

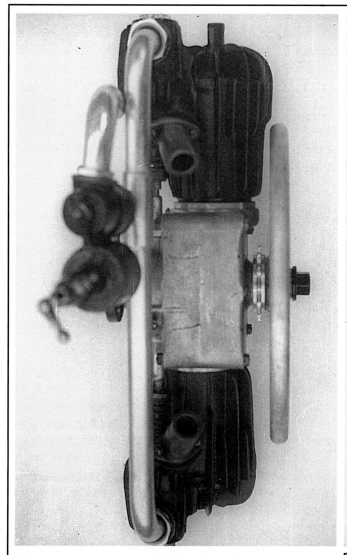

Three close-up photographs of Barter's compact 200cc engine which was retained by clips in what was basically a standard bicycle frame. This is an early example that pre-dates the engine unit shown in the preceding photograph. Surprisingly, it was found in New Zealand and it is certainly the earliest known example, probably made during 1905. The crankcase would have been cast in the Douglas Brothers foundry, which will explain how William Douglas became acquainted with Joseph Barter.

Opposite top: The only complete surviving example of the Fairy motorcycle, manufactured shortly before Barter's Light Motors Limited went into voluntary liquidation during 1907. It was found, completely dismantled and in a cardboard box, in a lighthouse on the east coast of Scotland! Rebuilt by Kevin Hellowell of Sowerby Bridge, West Yorkshire, it has since been ridden in a number of motorcycle events and also displayed at shows, with several awards to its credit. *(Photo: Halifax Evening Courier)*

Inset: The late Geoff Cheavin, a past Vice-President of the London Douglas Motor Cycle Club, with his 1912 2¾hp Douglas. The winner of many awards with this machine and a stalwart Club member, he bequeathed it to the Club so that it could be ridden by members in veteran and vintage events and not languish unused in a museum or a private collection. Note the period speedometer driven from the front wheel, not a legal requirement until many years after this machine was made.

Main picture: Riding in close company during the 1961 Banbury Run are Eric Brockway on his 1913 Ladies Model and the late Geoff Cheavin on his 1912 Model. It was on this occasion that Geoff was narrowly beaten for the award of the Percy Wheeler Memorial Trophy, which is presented to the entrant who has the highest total by adding together the age of the rider and that of his machine. Geoff's rival had been born just one day earlier! In those days there was no requirement to wear safety helmets.

Above: **A** rear carrier soon became a standard fitment on most machines, as is the case in this photograph of the rear end of a 1913 model. It provided a

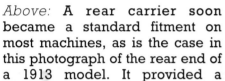

convenient means of carrying luggage or extra tools, and if a cushion was strapped to it, it could be adapted to carry a pillion passenger, sometimes mounted side-saddle!

Above right: A Klaxon horn was sometimes used in preference to the usual rubber bulb type. Of hefty dimensions and weight, this type of warning device was better suited to a car, but if it were mounted on one of the footboards of a motorcycle it was more secure and could be operated by the foot rather than by hand.

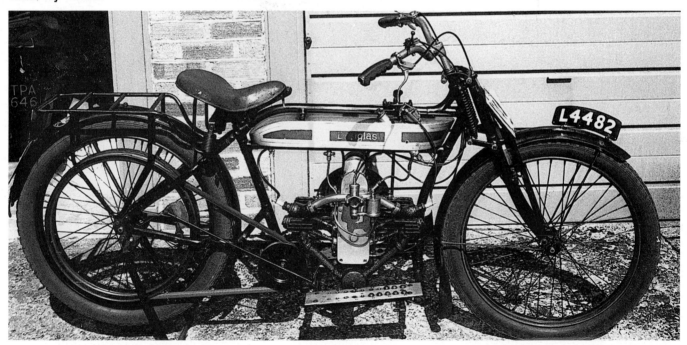

A complete off-side view of the 1913 model, another of the machines owned by Graeme Brown, with its Pioneer Run number still attached. A lower riding position was created by dropping the rear end of the top frame tube. From 1910 all models had featured a separate gearbox, initially two-speed, which was chain driven from the engine but drove the rear wheel by belt through a cross-over arrangement. The 'tram handle' gearchange level can be seen on the petrol tank.

Opposite top: Motorcycling was by no means the sole preserve of the male, even in the early days. Douglas was one of many manufacturers who made a special ladies' model, with a 'dropped' frame to accommodate a ladies' dress. This $2\frac{1}{4}$hp 1913 model was at one time owned by Eric Brockway, seen here, who rode it in the Sunbeam MCC's Pioneer Run from Tattenham Corner, Epsom, to Brighton from 1953 to 1971. The extra petrol tank seen to the rear of the main tank had beenadded specially for the run, to obviate the need to refuel en route. This model is fitted with a kickstarter to prevent need for an unladylike 'run and bump' start.

Left: Jill Savage of Farnborough, Hants, was another regular competitor in the Pioneer Run at one time, riding a similar model. Just 17 years old at the time when this photograph was taken she is seen getting her machine ready for the 1956 event, and it is interesting to reflect that the machine is 25 years older than its rider! There were five women competitors in that year's run, of which she was the youngest.

Above: Graeme Brown's much used 1914 model, fully equipped with a spare drive belt, leather toolboxes and handlebar-mounted bulb horn. Viewed from the nearside the exposed kickstarter and its ratchet can be seen, which engages with a pinion on the gearbox mainshaft. A Douglas was very easy to start such that a kickstarter required only the lightest of pressure. Those without this fitment were easily paddled away with both feet, after which the valve lifter was dropped to start the engine.

Top left: A close-up of this machine shows some nice period touches that include lace-up leather knee grips and an old-style licence holder retained by screws around its circumference. The curved front fork links are another Douglas characteristic; note how the side shields of the front mudguard will provide added protection from the often water-logged or muddy surface of the unmade roads of that era.

Top right: This offside close-up shows the hand-operated oil pump that draws oil to lubricate the engine from a separate oil compartment within the petrol tank. It is fed through a drip feed sight indicator on the tank top, immediately forward of the pump itself, from which the rate of flow can be regulated by an adjustable needle valve.

Main picture: Proof of use! Graeme Brown negotiates the roundabout that marks the start of the Crawley by-pass during the Sunbeam MCC's 1962 Pioneer Run. Obviously intent on keeping his 1914 model to schedule, he has a chronometer strapped to his left arm, as he is riding as a member of the London Douglas MCC team in a bid to win the Team Prize.

1916

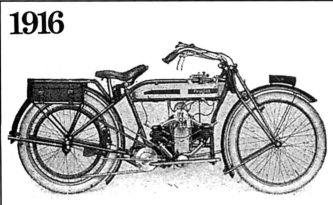

Model "U." 2¾ h.p., 2-speed Gear, £48; 3-speed Gear, £50

Model "V." 2¾ h.p., 2-speed Gear, £48; 3-speed Gear, £50

Model "W." 2¾ h.p., 3-speed Gear and Clutch - - £54

Surprisingly, the manufacture of motorcycles for the civilian market was permitted to continue until February 1917, despite the fact that Britain had been at war with Germany since 1914. Here is a reproduction of part of the announcement made by Douglas to introduce their 1916 models. A model fitted with leaf spring rear suspension was included in the announcement, but it never went into production.

W. A. Brace M.T.A.S.C., 2nd Sialkot Cavalry, F.A.V., Indian Ex. Force.—"After four months I am surprised at the marvellous stability and power of the 'Douglas.' It is absolutely grand."

A series of postcards were issued by the factory during the Great War to extol the virtues of the Douglas under active service conditions. These are two in the series, each with its own respective rider's testimonial. Many despatch riders seemed to prefer a Douglas to the alternative Triumph that also was supplied in large numbers.

"I am really satisfied with my 'Douglas,' and have done over 6,000 kilometres and never a stop. My machine is still as efficient as in November. Every day my engine is the admiration of many people. Bravo, for 'Douglas'!" writes C. A. de MONTIGNY,

Etat-Major de la 2nd Div. Armée Belge

Opposite top: A typical despatch rider and his Douglas mount, the latter in drab finish. Usually, tools were carried in a large wooden box permanently affixed to the rear carrier and the rider often carried a spare inner tube and drive belt wrapped around his person or attached to the machine itself. Note the mud shield fitted to the front down tube, to protect the forward facing sparking plug of the front cylinder.

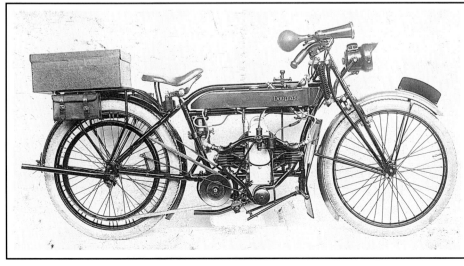

Left: A contemporary photograph of the 1918 WD Douglas in its khaki finish with the large box mounted on the rear carrier. In addition to the small leather-fronted toolbox suspended from the carrier on the right-hand side, two similar toolboxes are mounted on the left, suspended in similar fashion. The protective shield in front of the engine has a circular cut-out to aid engine cooling; note also the easy-to-operate centre stand, ineffective in the mud of Flanders.

A larger capacity 4hp model became available in 1915, designed primarily for use with a sidecar. Bore and stroke dimensions of 74.5 x 68mm gave a cubic capacity of 593cc. In common with the $2\frac{3}{4}$hp models it was fitted with the new three-speed gearbox that was then available after extensive testing.

After the war, motorcycle manufacturers strove to get back into the production of machines for the civilian market as quickly as possible, to meet an ever-increasing demand. Initially, the models they produced were almost identical to those they were making before production ceased of necessity in 1917. This is the Douglas stand at the first post-war Olympia Show of 1919, with a machine sold to Prince Albert in the foreground. It is inconceivable that members of the Royal Household would even consider riding motorcycles today, although a further warrant was granted in 1970 as suppliers of Vespa scooters and mopeds to HRH The Prince Philip, Duke of Edinburgh. It related to a commercial sidecar version used by the Royal Household to carry the Duke's polo equipment.

A factory photograph of the 1920 2¾hp model W20, which differed from its pre-war predecessor only in minor detail that comprised wider mudguards, a petrol tank with rounded edges and a stronger front fork of the welded, lugless type. It also had a Ferodo lined clutch in place of the former cork insert type – prone to slip through oil working its way onto the corks.

A close-up of the machine sold to Prince Albert, a 2¾hp model that has a soon-to-be-outmoded primitive stirrup-type front brake. This was the first of several Douglas motorcycles to be owned by His Royal Highness.

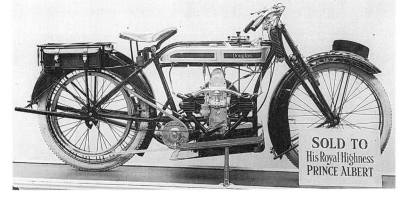

This and the following eight photographs illustrate in detail the various features of a typical 2¾hp Model B of the 1920s. This close-up of the nearside of the engine unit shows clearly the chain drive to the three speed gearbox, which has no provision for a clutch, the cylindrical expansion chamber of the exhaust system, the undertray to protect the engine from mud, water and general road debris and the British-made EIC magneto. Britain by now was making its own magnetos as the Great War had prevented the importation of German-made Bosch magnetos that were then in widespread use.

The offside of the engine unit showing the cross-over drive from the gearbox to the rear wheel by belt and pulley. Also shown is the slanting arrangement of the mechanically-operated side valves, with their tightly wound springs. The quality of the cylinder barrel casting is self-evident.

The belt pulley attached to the rear wheel is almost as large in diameter as the wheel itself. The same groove also doubles up as the rear braking surface for the identically angled brake block, actuated by a foot-operated pedal. The rear mudguard is well valanced and two leather-fronted toolboxes are attached to the rear carrier, of generous capacity.

A direct link with the pre-war models is the stirrup-type front brake, like that of a bicycle, relying on brake blocks being pulled against the wheel rim. Ineffective in the wet, they did little more than satisfy legal requirements. They soon removed the enamel from the rim, and if the brake blocks were allowed to work loose, they were inclined to rip out the wheel spokes. Note the side valances of the front mudguard.

The rear brake foot pedal is of sturdy dimensions, operating the rear brake block by means of a rod linkage. A clamp arrangement at its pivot point permits a range of adjustment, and a return spring ensures correct brake pull-off.

The welded girder-type front fork has its movement controlled by links and two strong springs. Note the screw-down grease-filled lubricators at the top of each spring pivot. Here, the front brake arrangement can clearly be seen.

The sight-feed of the hand pump lubrication system, from which the rider can observe, and if necessary adjust, the rate of oil flow. The needle-type adjuster is seen above the sight feed bowl, having a movable

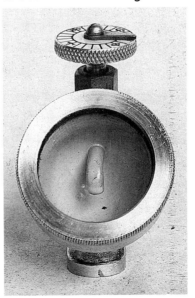

pointer to indicate the correct setting. Set into the top of the petrol tank it could momentarily divert the attention of the rider.

Above: The leather-fronted toolboxes, already mentioned, would have contained a set of good quality tools, sufficient for routine maintenance purposes and for minor roadside repairs in the event of a breakdown.

Left: A close-up of the front fork springing arrangement, which shows an additional grease-filled lubricator for the lower rear fork spindle. The telescopic arrangement of the front brake operating system can also be seen, and the Douglas steering head transfer used at this time.

This view of the Motor Shop within the Douglas factory was taken during February 1920. Sidecars wait to be attached to their respective machines whilst some of the solo machines on the benches await the installation of an engine and gearbox. Some idea of the vastness of the factory can be gained from this photograph.

With a light sprinkling of snow on the ground this photograph may well have been posed for publicity purposes as it shows the Clifton Suspension Bridge in the background, one of Bristol's most famous landmarks. A well set up sidecar outfit is probably the safest of all wheeled vehicles when road conditions become treacherous due to ice and snow.

21

A delightful period photograph of a group outside the Shoe Inn at North Wraxall, not far from Bristol along the A420, going east. They include one of the managers from the Douglas factory and the North Wraxall Postmaster. This public house is still frequented by motorcyclists today and has been the venue for several Vintage MCC gatherings.

Unfortunately the origin of this photograph remains unknown, although it is evident the driver of this 4hp Douglas combination and his lady passenger are taking part in some kind of competitive event – perhaps a road trial?

Fishing and a quiet picnic on the river bank provided yet another suitable topic for a publicity photograph that would exemplify the convenience of a motorcycle combination for recreational pursuits. Most probably this photograph and the one of the same couple on the right was taken on the banks of the River Avon. The machine has an early electric lighting set fitted.

The picturesque village of Castle Combe, just over the border in Wiltshire, forms the setting for this photograph of the early 1920s. Taken in wintertime the bareness of the trees accentuates the bleak effect of a dull, overcast day.

Overleaf: Another of the photographs taken in Castle Combe, the sidecar passenger now in conversation with one of the local shopkeepers. The coal cart pulled by the two heavy horses provides a memory of a bygone era.

Left: Yet another photograph with a piscatorial theme, but in a different location and with a different sidecar outfit, this time fitted with acetylene lighting. The fisherman seems to have a different girlfriend!

A day on the river affords an alternative means of enjoyment, providing the weather is fine. This shot was taken at Pilning, near Bristol, probably during the early spring, as indicated by the bare trees and the sidecar driver without his jacket. The machine is a 4hp model of the early 20s, fitted with a Douglas sidecar and electric lighting.

In this section of the Douglas factory, front forks are being assembled, each operator having his own welding torch and gas bottle. Working conditions in the twenties left a great deal to be desired for there is no evidence of a fire extinguisher or any means of ducting away the dangerous and unpleasant fumes. They must have made the working environment intolerable at times.

The Frame-Building Shop, which has a much better air of light and space about it. The frames here are being checked on bench-mounted jigs to ensure correct alignment, whilst to the right, wheels are being built within a separate enclosure.

A corner of the Final Assembly Shop, with its wooden benches and floor. They would have helped the great fire of several years later to take hold rapidly, the more so as they would have become grease and oil soaked over the years.

Above: Nearing completion in the Assembly Shop during 1922/3 is this line of machines on the left, most of which require the addition of their handlebar controls. On the right, customers' machines would appear to be in for minor repairs and/or attention, possibly under warranty. This is very much the era of acetylene lighting and footboards.

Left: His Royal Highness, Prince Albert, on one of his later purchases, a 1922 ohv model. It is fitted with an early design of disc brake.

Below: The International Six Days Trial is one of the most demanding of all competitive motorcycling events. In this undated and partially-faded photograph, two Douglas riders, Cliff King and J.J. Boyd-Harvey, are seen ascending Middle Down Hill near Shaftesbury on the first day's run from Southampton to Taunton.

A youthful Graeme Brown with his 1922 3½hp Sports Model at Brooklands, where he enjoyed a number of successes. Like the machine owned by Prince Albert it utilises the forerunner of today's widely accepted disc brake, a metallic disc on to which a pad lined with friction material pressed. On later disc brake models, this arrangement was reversed.

Taken during November 1922, this photograph depicts Jack Haslam, a very well known Douglas works rider and agent from Sheffield. He was associated with the Douglas marque for some 24 years. Here is an even better view of the early disc brakes. Jack was 6th in the 1913 Junior TT and in the 1922 TT had the doubtful distinction of being the oldest competitor.

PREVIOUS DOUGLAS SUCCESSES

	1912 JUNIOR RACE			Average Speed.
1. W. H. Bashall.	2¾ Douglas.	3h. 46m. 59s.	39·65.	
2. E. Kickham.	2¾ Douglas.	3h. 51m. 36s.		

1913 JUNIOR RACE

2. W. F. Newsome. 2¾ Douglas. 5h. 9m. 30s.

1923 JUNIOR RACE

3. A. H. Alexander. 3·46 Douglas. 4h. 9m. 35s.

SENIOR RACE

1. T. M. Sheard. 4 97 Douglas. 4h. 4m. 43s. 55·55.

SIDECAR RACE

1. F. W. Dixon. 5·96 Douglas. 2h. 7m. 48s. 53·15.

1924 SENIOR RACE

3. F. W. Dixon. 4·94 Douglas. 3h. 45m. 46s.

1925 SIDECAR RACE

1. L. Parker. 5·96 Douglas. 2h. 44m. 1,8s. 55·22.

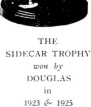

THE
SIDECAR TROPHY
won by
DOUGLAS
in
1923 & 1925

THE
JUNIOR TROPHY
won by
DOUGLAS
in
1912.

*Freddie Dixon and D. H. Denny, his passenger, on his 4 h.p.
Douglas outfit—winner of the 1923 Sidecar Race.*

Freddie Dixon, a very talented works rider and engineer, had the satisfaction of winning the first ever Sidecar TT of 1923 on this 596cc Douglas outfit, the banking sidecar being of his own design. His passenger was Walter Denny and his winning average speed 53.15mph. Freddie was employed by Douglas for a number of years and was the originator of some of the company's more successful designs. A win in the first ever Sidecar TT of 1923 and a further win in that year's Senior Race provided ample opportunity for good publicity. This page, taken from a later issue of the company's own magazine *Con Rod,* lists Douglas successes in the Isle of Man, which would always help to boost sales.

Freddie Dixon, in a suit and wearing a trilby hat, poses astride his 1923 banking sidecar outfit. Bearing the number 55, this outfit was the winner of the 1923 Sidecar TT Race, the first to be held in the Isle of Man.

Manxman Tom Sheard won the 1923 Senior TT on a 494cc Douglas at an average speed of 55.55mph, in weather conditions that were quite appalling. Jim Whalley on another 494cc Douglas put up the fastest lap at 59.74mph before he was forced to retire. These were very creditable performances bearing in mind it was pouring with rain throughout the race, with mist swirling around the Mountain. The drawing is from the Frontispiece on the 1924 Douglas catalogue.

The 2¾hp Touring Model OW of 1924. Rim brakes are still in general use, never particularly effective in the wet, and the gearbox remains mounted above the rear cylinder to help reduce the length of the wheelbase. The clutch is built into the outside exposed flywheel.

Above and following pages: **B. Santos from Spain rode a Douglas in the 1925 Senior TT,** as these two photographs confirm. In the first he is seen during a pit stop in the Glencrutchery Road, Douglas, whilst in the second he is at Hilberry after the long straight from Craig-ny-Baa.

Above: **A familiar name in the 1925 Senior TT was that of Gus Kuhn, who would soon make a name for himself during the early days of dirt track racing. He ran a motorcycle business too, in London, which changed its name only a comparatively short while ago.**

Facing page, top: **A view of the Douglas Depot workshops in the Isle of Man busy preparing entries for the 1925 TT. Freddie Dixon, wearing the tam-o-shanter hat, is working on Gus Kuhn's machine, whilst Cyril Pullin (wearing the trilby hat), and Bob Vaughan on his right, seem to be happy with what is going on. Freddie appears to be lifting the engine in or out of the frame.**

Facing page, bottom: **Another view of the Douglas Depot in the Isle of Man taken during 1925. Seated on the mudguard of the machine on the left is that year's Sidecar TT winner, Len Parker, with Cliff King next to him. Amongst the group standing are Eddy Withers, Bob Vaughan, Freddie Dixon and Cyril Pullin.**

Freddie Dixon was as good riding a solo machine as he was driving a sidecar outfit. Here he is seen rounding Ramsey Hairpin during a Senior TT of the mid '20s. He invariably rode without wearing goggles, which he would sling around his neck, although he did have a small screen mounted above the front racing number plate. He also preferred to use footboards.

This superb drawing by Grimes shows Sydney Flook on his way to victory in the 1927 Durban to Johannesburg race, a marathon event that was run over some 400 miles, mostly of rough terrain. It was the fifth successive win by a Douglas rider.

Douglas could offer in 1927 a lightweight sidecar designed to be attached to the 348cc EW model, or a deeper and more roomy single seat version suitable for attachment to any of the 600cc models. Both sidecars retailed at £14 and were well built.

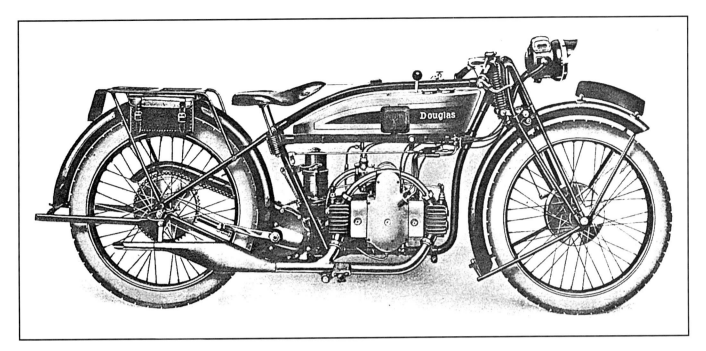

The Pullin-designed 348cc EW model represented a significant step-forward in Douglas design, especially after the initial teething troubles had been sorted out. These had been brought about by cutting corners in attempting to get the sale price down to an acceptable level. By 1927 the EW was proving a good, reliable mount and the Douglas trials team achieved success after success with it. Note the somewhat unusual gearchange through the centre of the petrol tank and the compactness of the side valve engine that now allows the gearbox to be mounted behind it.

A 600cc version also became available, primarily for sidecar use. Here seen is the Sports Model. If electric lighting was specified, a modified timing cover had attached a BTH pancake-type dynamo. For a publicity stunt, Harry Lorraine had himself handcuffed to an EW model before embarking on a 6,000 mile journey around the UK!

It is by no means uncommon for 'period' photographs to be filed uncaptioned and this is just one such example. It is worthy of inclusion since it shows William Douglas (left) observing some unknown check point in a road event. In all probability the rider of the machine that carries trade plates is taking part in a brake test, judging from the tyre marks on the road surface made by those who have passed through earlier.

Motorcycle football was very popular in the late twenties, as evidenced by this old and damaged photograph of a Douglas-sponsored team. Riders and venue unknown.

An historic photograph showing a dirt track model about to leave the factory incorporating Freddie Dixon's smaller, square airbox with built-in mechanical oil pump. Billy Dallison is seen seated on the machine and standing next to him a youthful Jack Parker, destined to be Britain's greatest speedway rider. The trio is made up by the inimitable Freddie Dixon.

Speedway, or dirt track racing as it was known initially, made its impact throughout Britain in 1928, after the first ACU-organised meeting at High Beech, in Epping Forest, proved an outstanding success. A Douglas was ideally suited to this form of racing and a special speedway model, the DT5, was soon evolved. This is a close-up of the engine unit of a machine painstakingly rebuilt by Len Cole, a foremost authority on these models.

A new speedway model leaves the Douglas works in 1928 complete with gauze shield in front of the engine to protect it from flying cinders. Only the bare essentials were fitted. The gearchange was kept locked in the one position, minor changes in ratio being effected by varying the size of the gearbox sprocket. Top gear ratio is usually 9:1. The rear wheel and its sprocket were made reversible, to help offset tyre wear on one side.

It is difficult now to remember that there were lady speedway riders too in the early days, some of whom were very successful. Among the foremost was Fay Taylour, possibly the best known of them all.

With the establishment of speedway tracks in most of Britain's provincial cities, as well as in the London suburbs, league racing soon came into vogue. Fixtures were organised along similar lines to those of football. This is the 1929 White City team comprising Ivor Hill, 'Hurricane' Hampson, 'Whirlwind' Baker, Jimmy Hindle (Captain, on machine), 'Champ' Upham, 'Lightning' Luke and 'Sunshine' Cannell.

Opposite top: The Stamford Bridge team of 1929 comprised Gus Kuhn (Captain), Wal Phillips, Bert Butt, Les Blakeborough, Fred Ralph and Colin Ford. All riding a dirt track Douglas, of course!

Opposite right: The Wembley Speedway team as they turned out in 1929. From left to right: Buster Frogley, Vic Deale, Bert Fairweather, Johnny Hoskins (Manager), Jack Johnson, Crawley Rous and Stan Catlett. The late Johnny Hoskins is regarded as the father of speedway racing as it was he who came up with the idea of racing on a loose surface, in Australia, in the mid-twenties.

Stamford Bridge Team

Douglas.

And they all ride Douglases !

Gus Kuhn, Wal Phillips, Bert Butt, Les Blakeborough, Fred Ralph, Colin Ford.

Above: 'Sprouts' Elder, perhaps the most consistent performer on the 'cinders', where he would sometimes be paid £100 a night in appearance money, a very large amount in those days. He earned a great reputation for his sportsmanship, as instanced at Stamford Bridge on 6th July, 1929. Faced with the option of running over fellow American Art Pechar (who had fallen in front of him) or taking to the safety fence flat out, he chose the latter, which cost him several fractured ribs and a few weeks in hospital. It was claimed his long legs gave him an advantage in a close finish if he stuck them straight out in front!

Famous personalities would often make guest appearances at speedway meetings. Here Teddy Baldock, a well-known boxer in 1929, sits on a dirt track Douglas owned by Jack Barnett, the latter of whom is providing the push start. Photographs such as this were specially posed; it is highly unlikely that Baldock actually rode the machine.

The road-going version of the dirt track Douglas was the SW5, which was fitted with brakes. In recent years, Bill Dent of the London Douglas MCC put up some surprisingly fast times at sprint meetings with this 1929 model SW6 (the 600cc version) he had rebuilt and prepared himself. Machines such as this were once described with some truth as 'looking fast whilst standing still'.

Another specially posed roadside photograph in which two Douglas riders (Cliff King and Eddy Withers) stop for a chat with their E29 600cc EWs. The lady sidecar passenger is busy picking flowers which then grew in abundance by the roadside.

Opposite top: The Douglas family were enthusiastic riders of their own product and not hesitant to enter for competition events either. Their participation was by no means restricted to the menfolk. Here, Irene and Rosina Douglas pose with their team-mate, Mrs Louie McLean, at the start of a Bristol Motor Cycle Club trial in which they comprised the formidable Ladies' Team.

Opposite bottom: Another shot of the Ladies' Team at the start of the Bristol Club's trial. Louie McLean (5) was one of the most successful of all lady trials riders, with many awards to her credit that included the special award for the Best Performance by a Lady Rider in the 1931 Scottish Six Days Trial.

Douglas enjoyed many overseas successes too. At the 1930 South African Durban to Johannesburg race, Douglas-mounted F.A.R. Zurcher (22) and Sydney Flook (21) started together and battled against each other during the whole of the 403 miles of the race. Zurcher crossed the finishing line only a wheel ahead of Flook, having recorded a time of 9 hours, 58 minutes and 37 seconds. He was placed ninth and Flook tenth. Of a total of 91 entries, only 22 finished, such was the severity of the course.

A favourite spot for taking publicity photographs was in the village of Cheddar, at the foot of the famous Gorge. Here, two Douglas riders and the sidecar passenger dally by the picturesque stream that runs alongside the road. Taken circa 1931, as evidenced by the Douglas tartan pattern around the petrol tank panels, there is a complete absence of other road traffic.

An imposing background is conveniently provided by this gateway, the West Entrance to Ashton Court, Long Ashton, near Bristol. Flat caps were seemingly then at the height of fashion amongst motorcyclists.

J.G.D. Phillips proudly displays the awards he has won with his 500cc ohv Douglas sidecar outfit during the years 1929-1932. Phillips and Sons of Dursley, Gloucestershire, had been Douglas agents since 1908 and won awards for window displays during the Dursley Traders' Association annual Shopping Week.

Enthusiasm for the Douglas motorcycle was by no means restricted to Britain alone. Here the Douglas Club of Basle, Switzerland, are seen clad in the authentic tartan of the Douglas clan.

Top: During the 'between the wars' period, officer cadets underwent training with various forms of wheeled and tracked vehicles. The Carden-Lloyd tracked vehicles seen here were the forerunners of the later and more familiar Bren Gun Carrier. The dispatch rider uses a Douglas, even though the army did not then order machines in large numbers from the Kingswood factory.

Bottom: The 350cc ohv model K32, typical of the machines being manufactured in 1932 at a time when the company was no longer owned by its founder. It was shortly to be faced with a financial crisis and the appointment of an Official Receiver. Hand gearchange still lingered on and with the high position of the gearbox it must have been difficult to use the kickstarter.

Following pages: On 22nd September 1932 Jim Douglas married Edith Prouse at St Mary's church, Bitton. Riders from the Douglas factory's Sports & Social Club formed a guard of honour on this happy occasion.

One of the more unusual projects undertaken by the new Douglas Motors (1932) Limited was the construction of the strange-looking Dynasphere, the brain child of a Dr J.A. Purves of Taunton. It was, in effect, a one-wheel vehicle designed to cross loose surfaces, such as sand. Powered by a B29 Douglas engine it was steered by the driver's seat sliding to the left or right. After extensive trials and being produced in a more sophisticated form, it proved impractical and the idea was subsequently abandoned.

FACING PAGE

Left: By 1933, William Douglas had re-purchased the company, largely with his own money, to save it from extinction. This advertisement, published in the 30th November 1933 issue of *The Motor Cycle* lists the models available for the 1934 season that now include a 150cc single cylinder two-stroke. Its cheapest version sold for £25.

Right: This close-up with the engine covers removed shows the separate dynamo, which has had its chain drive removed for reasons unknown. Also in view is the Villiers carburettor and the clutch of the three-speed Albion gearbox. The primary chain has only a short run and in consequence it wore rapidly.

Bottom: The early 150cc two-strokes, subsequently given the name Bantam, used a proprietary Villiers engine in a horizontal position. In this photograph the cylinder head can just be seen. A flywheel magneto was located beneath the 'saucepan lid' on the offside, although the lighting was powered by a separate, chain-driven dynamo. Note the large diameter front brake, from another model in the Douglas range.

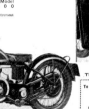
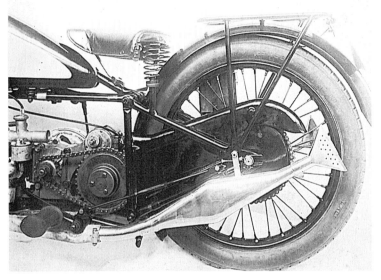

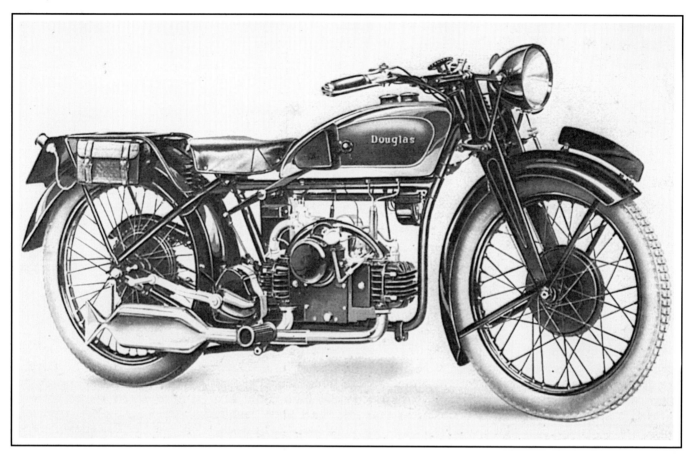

It was anticipated that a 250cc twin, the Comet, would be available in 1934 but it was never put on the market. It was to have used the pressed steel front fork specified for the Bantam two-stroke and also the large diameter front brake.

The 1934 model Z34 750cc twin, the only model to retain the twin front down tube frame. Seen with the machine is Billy Latchem, a well-known Douglas competition rider at that time.

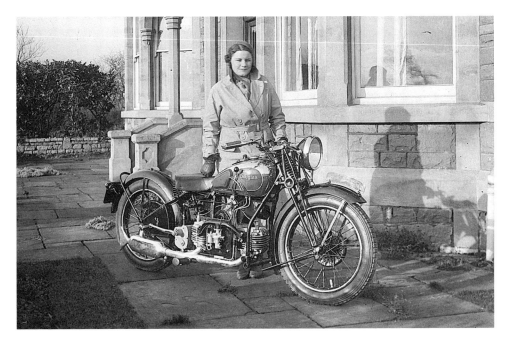

Left: The two daughters of the Douglas family, Irene and Rosina, were keen motorcyclists too and frequently took part in competition events. Here Rosie Douglas poses with a 1935 500cc Blue Chief model, the engine unit of which was used to power the transverse engine Endeavour model.

Below: Douglas created quite a sensation with their transverse-engined Endeavour model, designed by Eddy Withers and Jack Clapham. What started initially as a design for a 250cc model, the Golden Star, ended up as this 494cc machine, based on the Blue Chief engine. It featured shaft drive and a four-speed gearbox, with a kickstarter that operated BMW fashion.

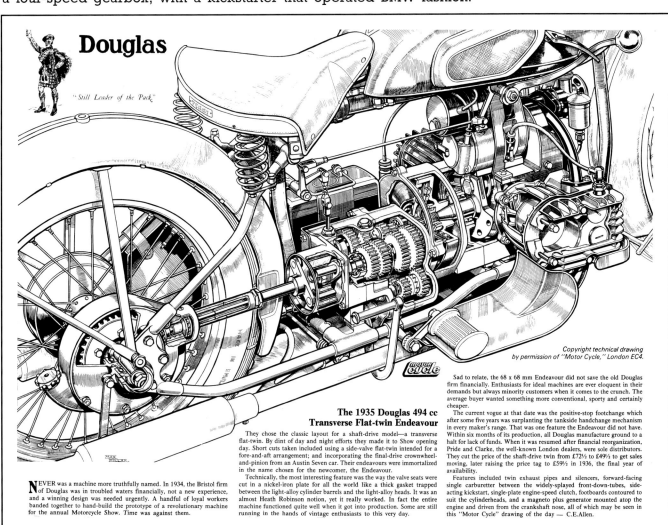

Douglas

"Still Leader of the Pack"

Copyright technical drawing by permission of "Motor Cycle," London EC4.

The 1935 Douglas 494 cc Transverse Flat-twin Endeavour

They chose the classic layout for a shaft-drive model—a transverse flat-twin. By dint of day and night efforts they made it to Show opening day. Short cuts taken included using a side-valve flat-twin intended for a fore-and-aft arrangement; and incorporating the final-drive crownwheel-and-pinion from an Austin Seven car. Their endeavours were immortalized in the name chosen for the newcomer, the Endeavour.

Technically, the most interesting feature was the way the valve seats were cut in a nickel-iron plate for all the world like a thick gasket trapped between the light-alloy cylinder barrels and the light-alloy heads. It was an almost Heath Robinson notion, yet it really worked. In fact the entire machine functioned quite well when it got into production. Some are still running in the hands of vintage enthusiasts to this very day.

NEVER was a machine more truthfully named. In 1934, the Bristol firm of Douglas was in troubled waters financially, not a new experience, and a winning design was needed urgently. A handful of loyal workers banded together to hand-build the prototype of a revolutionary machine for the annual Motorcycle Show. Time was against them.

Sad to relate, the 68 x 68 mm Endeavour did not save the old Douglas firm financially. Enthusiasts for ideal machines are ever eloquent in their demands but always minority customers when it comes to the crunch. The average buyer wanted something more conventional, sporty and certainly cheaper.

The current vogue at that date was the positive-stop footchange which after some five years was surplanting the tankside handchange mechanism in every maker's range. That was one feature the Endeavour did not have. Within six months of its production, all Douglas manufacture ground to a halt for lack of funds. When it was resumed after financial reorganization, Pride and Clarke, the well-known London dealers, were sole distributors. They cut the price of the shaft-drive twin from £72½ to £49½ to get sales moving, later raising the price tag to £59½ in 1936, the final year of availability.

Features included twin exhaust pipes and silencers, forward-facing single carburetter between the widely-splayed front-down-tubes, side-acting kickstart, single-plate engine-speed clutch, footboards contoured to suit the cylinderheads, and a magneto plus generator mounted atop the engine and driven from the crankshaft nose, all of which may be seen in this "Motor Cycle" drawing of the day — C.E.Allen.

Two views of the Endeavour model of 1935. Although it was well reviewed in the motorcycling press and much talked about amongst motorcyclists in general, when it came to purchase the latter remained as conservative as ever and very few chanced their money. Only about 50 were sold. The company's hoped for breakthrough never occurred and by mid-1935 it was again in financial difficulties, with the result that all connections with its founder were severed for good.

Above: A close-up of the Endeavour engine unit. An unusual feature of the engine was a detachable plate between the cylinder barrel and head that carried the valve seats. It was the subject of British Patent 430,274.

Reg Bryant, seen here seated on an Endeavour, was one of the faithful few who had seen long service with Douglas, through both good and bad times. When he retired in 1967 he had been with the company for 49 years, latterly as Chief Draughtsman and also Service Manager.

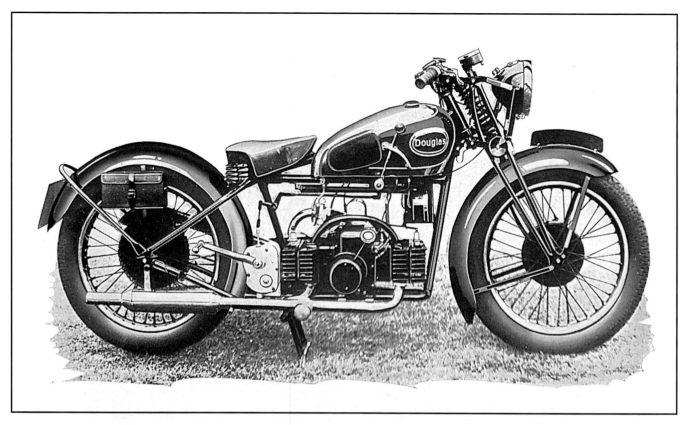

Now owned by Aero Engines Limited, Douglas had been bought in the hope that production space would be available for the manufacture of Hispano-Suiza aircraft engines they expected to build under licence. The contract was never awarded them so they continued to manufacture motorcycles, mostly assembled from spare parts already in stock. This is an artist's impression of the DC/38 600cc twin from their 1938 catalogue, for sale at £62.10s.

Aero Engines Limited had expected to market another, quite different, lightweight two-stroke, the model CL/38 of 150cc capacity. Like one or two other projected designs of the past, it never went into production. This is an artist's impression, also from the 1938 catalogue. It was the only other model they listed.

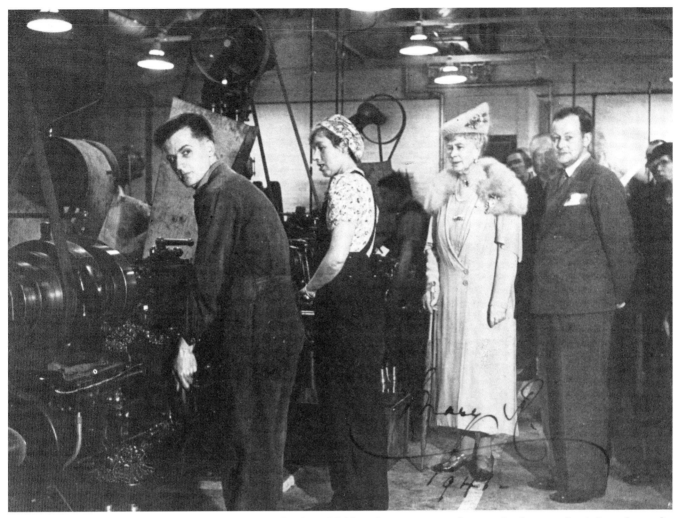

Queen Mary visited the Douglas factory during 1941, when war work was being undertaken largely for the Ministry of Aircraft Production. It is unusual for a member of the Royal Family to sign a photograph as is seen here.

This interesting drawing produced by Reg Bryant on 1st May 1939 shows some remarkable similarities with the models that were produced after World War 2, especially with regard to the layout of the engine unit. Note the unusual mode of brake operation, not unlike that adopted by Girling.

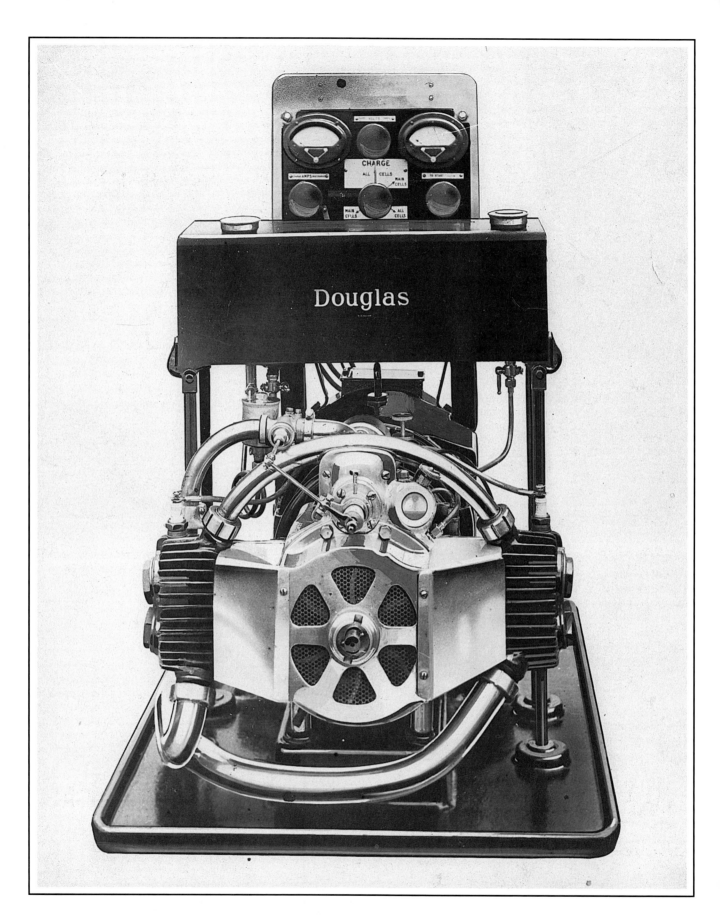

It should not be forgotten that Douglas made a wide variety of stationary engines and had been doing so prior to the 1914-18 war. Here is a typical example coupled to a dynamo, to provide a portable means of supplying electrical power on site. Note how the carburettor is connected to the governor to ensure the dynamo is run at constant speed.

An aerial view of the Douglas works in Kingswood, showing the extensive sports ground on the right. The original multi-storey office block is evident in the foreground, fronting on to Hanham Road. The sports ground has since become a company car park and also accommodates a further extension to the works, but there is still an active sports and social club on site.

A little-known model is the DV60, a prototype which was made with a view to military use. The basic requirements called for an engine of 600cc capacity, a maximum speed of 70mph, fuel consumption of not less than 70mpg and for the machine to be inaudible at 400 yards. The project was eventually abandoned, only to be resurrected several years later when the Douglas, a BSA and a Triumph, all prototypes, competed in the 1948 Scottish Six Days Trial with army riders. By then, a post-war Radiadraulic front fork had been added, with matching wheel and mudguard. Note the fully enclosed rear chain drive and the saddle with its sprung telescopic pillar. The machine is now owned by Graeme Brown.

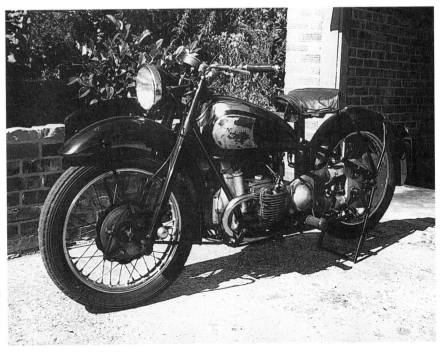

A total of 2,234 models, dating from 1947, carry the now familiar T/35 engine and frame prefix lettering and numbers, all of them manufactured at the Kingswood Works. Of these, over 100 are recorded in the Register of the London Douglas MCC, still in existence today. A combination of transverse mounted engine, torsion bar rear suspension and Radiadraulic front forks enabled the company to advertise a machine that 'Made Douglas different'. This somewhat out-of-focus publicity photograph of an early T35 model shows the specially made-up front number plate – Douglas Kingswood Bristol 350cc.

A batch of the early post-war T35 models was shipped to South America as part of the export drive. Here, Raul Jarret Barros of Santiago, Chile, has converted one into racing trim by removing most of the non-essential items and fitting megaphone exhausts. All the post-war Douglas twins reverted to a transversely-mounted engine unit and with the exception of the competition models, utilised an ingenious torsion bar rear suspension system.

Overleaf: The old and the new, a nicely staged photograph taken during the Sunbeam MCC's annual rally at Newlands Corner, near Guildford, in 1948. The 1913 2¾hp model is ridden by Fred Lacey, who had owned it since new, and the 1948 Sports Model by F.J. Poppe, the son of one of the Douglas Directors who was much involved with the design of the original T35 model.

Many consider the best of all the post-war models to have been the 1948/9 Sports Model with its upswept exhaust pipes and 'straight through' Burgess silencers that gave it a very sonorous exhaust note. For a time it was the fastest 350 on the road, with a maximum speed of 78mph. This is a 1949 model.

Three members of the London Douglas MCC entered for the 1949 Junior Clubmans TT, riding the much improved Mark III models. The rider here is Tony Camfield who, despite his second lap time being faster than that of the other Douglas entrants, was soon forced to retire. Franz Pados, who had been entered by the Douglas works, finished 16th at an average speed of 70.28mph. Jack Hill was 35th at 66.39mph and W.F. Wood 50th at 61.90mph.

Before the use of more modern transmission of press photographs it was not uncommon for two-wheel transport to be used. Douglas enthusiast Eddy Withers, the 'boss' of Withers of West Norwood Limited, is seen here astride a Mark III Sports Model, with fellow employees Ted Brigginshaw and Albert Le Roy on Standard Models, about to return to base. They are carrying press photographs rushed from a London athletics meeting to a waiting Air France Lockheed.

Jeff Clew's 1948 Mark III Model, which was rescued from the ultimate fate. It was found after children had ridden it around a field until it would run no longer and had then set it on fire. After mainly superficial cosmetic attention, it has since covered a further 12,000 miles and is still going strong on its original crankshaft and big ends.

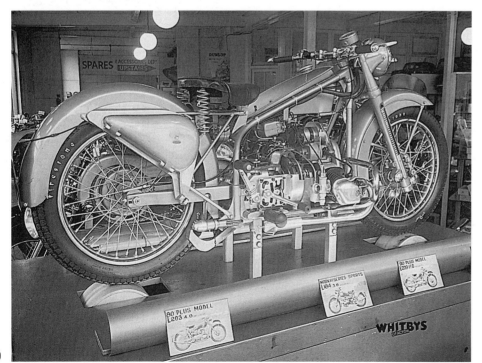

The Mark V Model was introduced in November 1950, resplendent in its distinctive polychromatic blue finish. The capacious toolboxes, one on each side of the machine, had originated on the intermediate Mark IV model and carried an extension on which the pillion footrests were mounted. Previously the latter had been attached to the swinging arm fork and therefore rose and fell with it. This sectioned model formed part of a window display at Whitby's of Acton, a West London dealer long associated with the Douglas marque. Today sectioned machines such as this seem to be a lost art.

Above: An artist's impression of what was to have been the 'standard' Mark V Model, featuring the earlier 'woffle box' silencer and semi-straight handlebars fitted with an internal twist grip. This and the following two illustrations formed part of the Douglas catalogue entitled 'Shipshape and Bristol Fashion'.

Overleaf top: The production version of the Mark V Model, had separate silencers of Burgess manufacture and raised handlebars fitted with the usual type of twist grip. The front mudguard mounting was not very satisfactory and formed a constant source of complaint.

Overleaf bottom: The 80 Plus model was finished in a distinctive maroon colour and was, in effect, a 'failed' 90 Plus model in that the power output of the engine was below the 25bhp at 6,500rpm norm. Fitted with a wider ratio gearbox it made a much more flexible high performance road machine. Few 80 Plus models were ever raced.

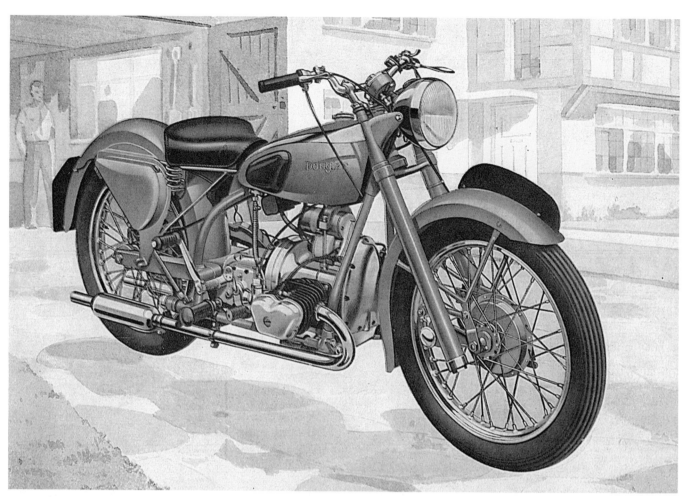

Great excitement was created by the debut of the 90 Plus Model at the 1949 Show, its designation relating to its performance capabilities. It could be supplied in full racing trim with a number of optional extras or alternatively, fully equipped for use on the road. It was finished in a gold colour.

A nicely restored example of the 90 Plus model in full racing trim which can be seen in the Sammy Miller Museum at New Milton, Hants. Purchased in somewhat neglected condition, it was restored to its present pristine condition by the Museum.

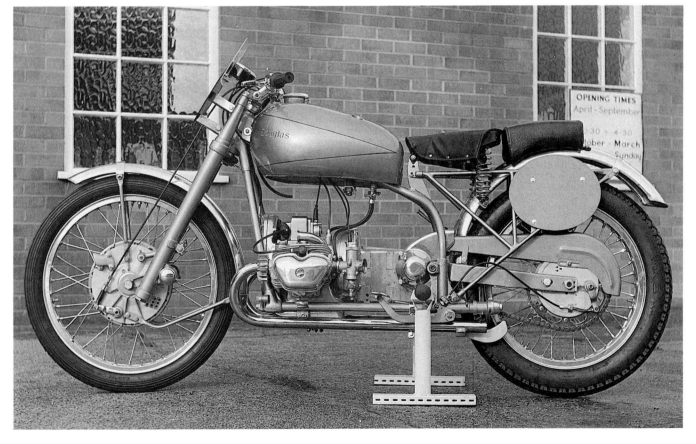

DISTRIBUTORS

ROOTES GROU

MOTOR | CARS

LAYTON

LAYTONS

Photograph previous pages: A massive gathering of members of the London Douglas MCC outside Laytons of Oxford, dealers in the Douglas marque. Although most of the riders are no longer associated with the Club, a few of their machines are still in existence and recorded on the Club Register.

The rigid frame Competition Model was built only in small numbers and enjoyed but a brief spell of existence. This group, taken outside the Kingswood works, comprises (left to right): Charles Ball, Ivor Bailey, Ted Townsend, Ted Breffitt (works rider, seated on bike), Charlie Mein, Rex Walker, Eddy Withers and Franz Pados.

This shot, taken during the 1950 International Six Days Trial held in Wales, shows Ted Brefitt leading Eric Cheney through the Abergwesyn watersplash in mid-Wales. As can be seen, he is riding a specially-prepared machine complete with competition tyres, torsion bar rear suspension and full lighting equipment. The downswept exhaust pipes could well have proved a handicap.

A rear view of the Douglas team that entered the Swedish Six Days Trial of 1951 and eventually took the third team prize. They too are riding spring frame models equipped with lighting that have the advantage of an upswept exhaust system and competition tyres.

The late Claude McCormack, who played a leading role in the revival of the company during the '50s and '60s. It was he who foresaw great possibilities for the Vespa scooter in Britain and was instrumental in arranging for its manufacture under licence at Kingswood, which led to a 'boom' in scooters. His name is perpetuated in an annual road trial event organised by the Bristol Section of the London Douglas MCC.

It was customary for celebrities to be present at new model launches, as in the case here where Charmain Innes, of stage, radio and TV fame, attended the production line launch of the 90 Plus model at the Kingswood factory. In those days models wore clothes, but the subject of the joke remains unknown.

Of all machines, the 90 Plus model would seem to be highly inappropriate for racing on ice, if only because the angle of lean would ground the right-hand rocker cover. The rider is Bertil Hagstrom of Stockholm.

This close-up of Hagstrom's machine shows the vicious-looking steel spikes that are fitted to each tyre in order to maintain grip. Needless to say, safety guards are required to cover a large area of the circumference of both wheels. If a rider is unfortunate enough to slide off, as often happens, the consequences of his bike catching up with him can be imagined.

Overleaf: **Clubs for enthusiastic Douglas owners had been established all over the world. Here members of the Douglas Club of Basel and Umbebung, Switzerland, are seen with their Mark models, providing a useful form of publicity that would be of value in the company's export drive.**

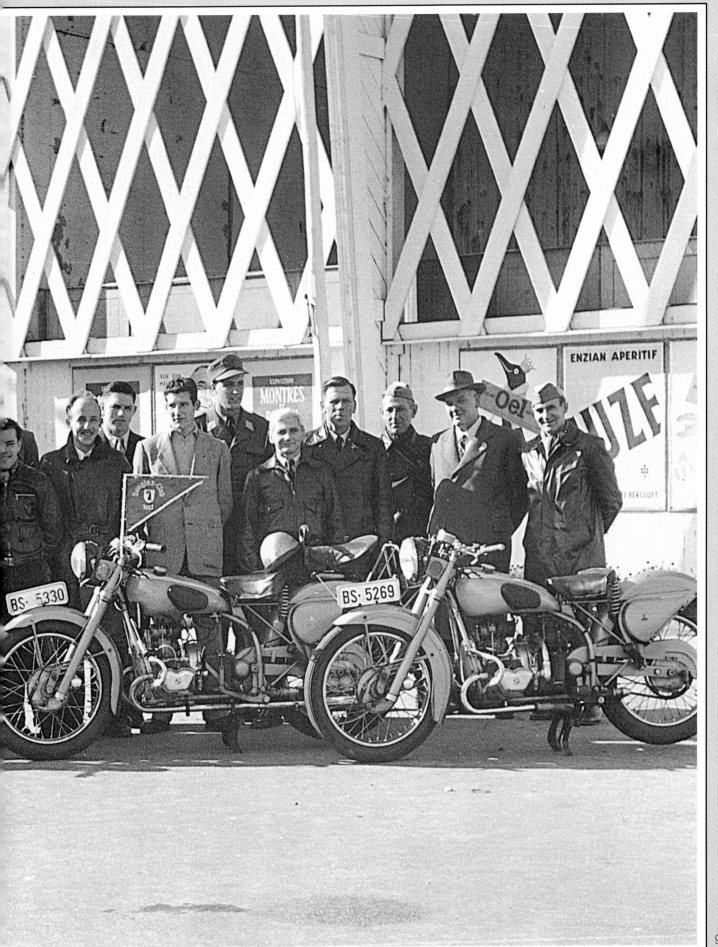

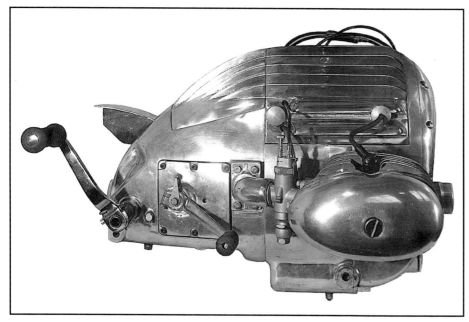

The handsome-looking power unit of the prototype 500cc twin. As can be seen, some of its features were incorporated in the later Dragonfly model. Ignition was by Lucas Magdyno, which is hidden under the detachable finned cover.

Another machine that had attracted a great deal of attention at the 1951 Motor Cycle Show was the prototype 500cc twin, to which was attached a Watsonian single seat sidecar. It would have provided the answer to those who required the additional power for either solo or sidecar use, but sadly there was not the money available for its development and in consequence it never went into production. Note the use of a Plus series front brake and similarities with the standard 350cc Mark models. Eric Brockway was able to save it from being broken up and it is now in solo form with his collection of Douglas memorabilia.

On occasions, overseas motorcycling clubs would visit the Kingswood factory by prior arrangement, where they were made very welcome and given a conducted tour of the factory premises. This group are members of the Douglas Club of Switzerland, seen assembled outside the Hanham Road offices.

Today, there is a need to train learner motorcyclists before they can obtain a licence and ride on the road. The Douglas company were loyal supporters of the old RAC/ACU Training Scheme and over many years they supplied machines to the RAC for use by learners under the joint ACU scheme. On occasions they were presented at the company but this 1952 handing-over ceremony was at a Bristol school, involving a 125cc Vespa scooter and a Mark V Model.

The expressions on the faces of some of the schoolboys attending a sports day at their Filton school clearly show they thought it a joke that Douglas at one time made a model for lady riders. Filton is, of course, the home of the famous Brabazon and Concorde aircraft. The photograph was taken in the early sixties.

The Dragonfly, the last model to be made by Douglas, was displayed at the 1954 Earls Court Show. As will be seen, the theme of precision engineering was exemplified by the giant micrometer, with a Dragonfly model between its jaws. Like its predecessors, the Dragonfly was of 350cc capacity.

It is not generally known that one of the earliest (1907) engines made by Douglas was a vee four. One has survived and after much work by Freddie Dixon and Eddy Withers it was installed in the frame and cycle parts of a veteran twin so that it would be eligible to take part in Pioneer Runs. At the 1958 Motor Cycle Show it became indirectly the centre of attraction when one of the Latin Quarter show girls posed on it whilst visiting the Douglas stand with Tommy Trinder.

Freddie Dixon enjoying a night out with friends at the 1954 BEMSEE Dinner. Seated on his right is his wife Dolly, whilst standing opposite wearing glasses is a young-looking Eddy Withers, for many years Freddie's assistant. On the extreme right with drink in hand and cigarette is an even younger-looking Graeme Brown.

Although Eddy Withers never accepted the Vespa scooter as a new mode of transport, his interest was such that his company was successful in selling many thousands. This 'special', adapted for the distribution of the London Evening Standard newspaper to street vendors, was one of many versions that appealed to fleet users.

When Douglas ceased production of motorcycles, Graeme Brown acquired their huge stock of spare parts which he transferred to his business premises in Meadrow, Godalming. This photograph shows Graeme with some of his well-stocked spares bins, which have helped innumerable Douglas owners keep their machines on the road or to restore those that have lain neglected to full running order.

Part of the 50th Anniversary of the London Douglas MCC coincided with a speedway meeting at Eastville Stadium, Bristol, on 15th September, 1978, in which a race was included in the programme for vintage speedway bikes, sponsored by Douglas (Sales & Service) Ltd. Several dirt track Douglas models took part, and seen here with two of Len Cole's immaculate machines are (left to right): William Douglas II (72), Ern Edwards (78), Howard Guest (74), Ray Cordy (London Douglas MCC) and Len Parker (78), winner of the 1925 Sidecar TT on a Douglas and one-time speedway rider himself.

Previous page: Henry Body, a former South West Centre grasstrack sidecar champion, won the vintage race in convincing style, on John Hill's dirt track Douglas. He was presented with the original silver helmet and gauntlets that were taken out of storage specially to mark this historic occasion.

100 YEARS OF ENGINEERING ACHIEVEMENT AT KINGSWOOD.

A commemoration by Bendix Limited.

On 13th July 1985 Bendix Limited, the present occupiers of the old Douglas premises in Kingswood, decided to commemorate 100 years of engineering achievement in Kingswood with a civic reception. A handsome limited edition commemorative booklet, as shown, was specially produced for the occasion, heavily illustrated and containing a great deal of information about Douglas. Although no Douglas motorcycles were made after March 1957, it is pleasing that its successors have recognised the high regard with which this once famous name is still acknowledged locally and have helped preserve its memory in such a tangible manner.

Previous page top: The Bendix premises were made available to members of the London Douglas MCC for a display of their machines that covered virtually the whole of the 50 year span of manufacture. The machine in the foreground is a 1913 Ladies' Model.

Previous page bottom: This 'Red Devil' dirt track Douglas is a very rare machine, owned by Henry Body. It is a special high performance version of the standard dirt track model finished in red and silver, prepared and tuned by Bert Dixon (the speedway engine tuner) to give a power output of 34.5bhp. Its engine was run whilst on display at Bendix, to the delight of many of the visitors.

Seen here, gathered around an EW Model on display at the Bendix premises, are (left to right) Graeme Brown, Ray Cordy and Jeff Clew, of the London Douglas MCC. Jeff is the author of *The Douglas Motorcycle: The Best Twin*, a complete history of Douglas, which was first published in 1974.

Previous pages: John Hill with his 1928 Dirt Track Douglas at the Bendix gathering, the machine ridden by Henry Body when he won the vintage race at Bristol Speedway. John is a leading expert on the Douglas marque and readers of this book will be indebted to him for checking the accuracy of the photograph captions. *(Photo: Bristol United Press)*

In 1987, Henry Body achieved the remarkable speed of over 111mph at Colerne, electronically recorded, on this 1929 600cc Douglas he had built and tuned himself, in weather conditions that were anything but ideal. Seen with him in this photograph is William Douglas III, the great, great grandson of the founder, who is a keen enthusiast and also a member of the London Douglas MCC.

Another very famous racing machine is this 1926 494cc Isle of Man Replica model which was purchased secondhand from the Douglas showrooms in London during 1929 by Dr. Joseph Bayley. It has been on loan to Len Cole since 1948, a leading Douglas Exponent who not only has looked after it but also has provided riders of the calibre of Howard German, Barry Briggs, George Brown and Mike Coombes. It averaged 90mph over the Standing Start Kilometre at Brighton in 1977 and in 1978 won the *Moto Revue* cup at Le Mans during La Coupe de l'Age d'Or event. Dr. Bayley is seen seated on the machine, with Len Cole on the right and Phil Manzano in between them, in a typical paddock shot at the September 1987 Brighton sprint. Concessions to performance have been made in the form of a Norton gearbox and Amal Concentric carburettors.

To celebrate the Diamond Jubilee of the London Douglas Motor Cycle Club, members returned to the birthplace of this famous marque at Kingswood for a Douglas Cavalcade over the weekend of the 19th/21st August 1988. It was organised by the Bristol Section of this world-famous Club, with the full co-operation of Kingswood Borough Council who kindly provided the facilities.

The weekend opened on the Friday evening with some 250 members attending a questions and answers session at the Kingswood Civic Centre. Jeff Clew, Ray Cordy, John Hill and Eddy Withers sat on the panel of experts to answer the questions.

Saturday saw the grand cavalcade of Douglas machines travel a 25 mile route which the factory testers used. In the evening a full house assembled in the old Douglas Works Social Club, by courtesy of Bendix Ltd.

On the Sunday, preceded by a civic reception, the biggest display of Douglas machines ever seen was on view in Kingswood Park. Models from the earliest production in 1907 until the cessation of production in 1957 could be seen.

These four photographs, published by courtesy of the Editor of the LDMCC magazine *The New Conrod*, show part of the outside display of machines. Inside the huge marquees was another display of some of the concours machines and stationary engines.

Four Douglas stalwarts meet up at the 1988 Douglas Cavalcade. Left to right: Graeme Brown, a Douglas agent since 1926, Eddy Withers, whose association with Douglas goes back to 1925, Eric Brockway, who joined Douglas in 1949 and remained with them until his retirement in 1982, and Ern Hendy, son of Ern Hendy Senior, himself a former Douglas employee. Ern Junior joined Douglas after leaving school and is currently with the present distributors of the Vespa scooter in the UK.

Percy Radford, of Westbury-on-Trym, near Bristol, astride his 1932 Model G 600cc Douglas, about to start in the 1989 Banbury Run organised by the Vintage MCC. Percy has been a regular competitor in this annual event for many years.

This quite charming print was resurrected by Percy Radford and used as the subject for his 1989 personal Christmas card. It shows a parson tending his flock at Spring Farm, Dundry, a village to the south of Bristol. The parson's mount is a 1927 ohv sidecar outfit and it is difficult to imagine a more rural scene.

Though Douglas never produced a 'Dragonfour', Douglas enthusiast Don Brown, a member of the Bristol Section of the London Douglas MCC, has constructed this 700cc four cylinder version of the twin cylinder Dragonfly after three years' painstaking work. When making its first public showing at the 1990 Bristol Classic Motorcycle Show, Don won the 'Non Standard – Non Production Machine' trophy, and at the Stafford International Classic Bike Show, the *Classic and Motorcycle Mechanics* trophy for the 'Machine of Most Technical Merit'.

Eric Brockway at his desk during the days of Douglas (Sales and Service) Ltd., at the Fishponds Trading Estate, Bristol.

Douglas Fades Out

The end of Douglas (Sales and Service) Limited, the remaining sales and marketing part of the old company, came on 30th June 1982, following the acquisition of the UK Vespa distribution by Two Four Accessories. As a result, Vespa (UK) Limited came into being, a Heron Corporation Company, with premises in Crawley, West Sussex.

Eric Brockway, who had been in charge of Douglas (Sales and Service) for many years, announced his retirement at the same time. In a letter dated 23rd June sent to all Vespa dealers he took the opportunity to announce a farewell to Douglas management that indicated also his intention to retire and his regrets in having to do so after a stewardship that had extended over a period of almost 33 years. He expected the changeover to take three months to effect and he thought now was the opportune time to depart. In his letter he said "I earnestly wish the new enterprise, and every single dealer concerned, all good fortune".

In summarising his long period of service with Douglas, Eric Brockway wrote "The mutual understanding of our distributor-dealer relationship has provided the foundation of the success we have achieved in the past and will serve as a good foundation at this time of change to give fresh impetus in meeting the challenges and conditions of today's market place". That was the essential Eric, always looking ahead and having confidence in the future, and not forgetting those who had offered such loyal and faithful service in the past.

111

The London Douglas Motor Cycle Club

Believed to be the only motorcycle club in the world that caters exclusively for owners of Douglas motorcycles and those that have an interest in them, the London Douglas Motor Cycle Club is by no means London-based as its title implies. Now an International Club, it has a world-wide membership, with active sections in many countries as well as throughout the United Kingdom.

Formed in 1928 by a group of keen, London-based Douglas enthusiasts, the Club enjoyed an active membership interested in camping, rallies, and sporting events of various kinds. It had its own magazine too, entitled 'Con-Rod', a high quality magazine-type of presentation that was fostered by the company for a number of years. When war was declared in 1939, the Club's activities were suspended 'for the duration' and its trophies put into store for safe keeping.

After the War the Club was re-formed by seven of its pre-war members, and its membership grew steadily until the manufacture of Douglas motorcycles ceased during 1957. Somehow the Club managed to keep going throughout the lean years that followed, a persistence that ultimately was rewarded by an upturn in membership that commenced during the mid 1960s. At the time of going to press membership is in excess of 750 and it is likely to continue increasing as more old machines are found and restored.

Members are kept informed of Club activities through a bi-monthly magazine entitled *The New ConRod*. They comprise all manner of pursuits ranging from social gatherings to competitive events of various kinds, the high spot of the year being the Club's Gymkhana/Rally which is currently held each June in the Bicester area. Machines are kept running by an excellent Spares Scheme which applies to both the pre- and post-war models. Where problems have been encountered with parts no longer available and there has been sufficient demand, the Club has had pattern parts made to a high standard on a limited production basis. There is also a Machine Register which is regularly updated so that a record is maintained of machines owned by members, and provision for answering technical enquiries or giving general advice.

Currently (1990), the Membership Secretary is Reg Holmes, of 48 Standish Avenue, Stoke Lodge, Patchway, Bristol, BS12 6AG (Telephone 0454 613653) who will be able to provide more detailed information about the Club and its activities. For anyone who owns a Douglas motorcycle or who is generally interested in the marque, membership of the Club becomes an essential requirement.